TULSA CITY COUNTY LIBRARY

P9-APO-701

MRJC

MAR 2018

THE PROBLEM WITH
EARLY
COMPUTERS

oOPs!

BY RYAN NAGELHOUT

 Gareth Stevens
PUBLISHING

Please visit our website, www.garethstevens.com. For a free color catalog of all our high-quality books, call toll free 1-800-542-2595 or fax 1-877-542-2596.

Library of Congress Cataloging-in-Publication Data

Nagelhout, Ryan.
  The problem with early computers / Ryan Nagelhout.
      pages cm. — (Bloopers of invention)
  Includes bibliographical references and index.
  ISBN 978-1-4824-2772-1 (pbk.)
  ISBN 978-1-4824-2773-8 (6 pack)
  ISBN 978-1-4824-2774-5 (library binding)
  1. Computers—History—Juvenile literature. I. Title.
  QA76.23.N34 2016
  004.09—dc23

                                    2015008466

First Edition

Published in 2016 by
Gareth Stevens Publishing
111 East 14th Street, Suite 349
New York, NY 10003

Copyright © 2016 Gareth Stevens Publishing

Designer: Sarah Liddell
Editor: Ryan Nagelhout

Photo credits: Cover, p. 1 Bertrand LAFORET/Contributor/Gammo-Rapho/Getty Images; p. 5 Tom Kelley Archive/Stringer/Archive Photos/Getty Images; p. 7 (abacus) Ti Santi/Shutterstock.com; p. 7 (quipu) Claus Ableiter/Wikimedia Commons; p. 9 (Pascal) DEA PICTURE LIBRARY/De Agostini Picture Library/Getty Images; p. 9 (calculator) NYPL/Science Source/Science Source/Getty Images; p. 11 (Babbage) Materialscientist/Wikimedia Commons; p. 11 (Difference Engine) UniversalImagesGroup/Contributor/Universal Images Group/Getty Images; p. 13 (Z1) Topory/ Wikimedia Commons; p. 13 (Z3) Jahoe/Wikimedia Commons; p. 15 Bletchley Park Trust/Contributor/ SSPL/Getty Images; p. 17 (UNIVAC) Education Images/UIG/Universal Images Group/Getty Images; p. 17 (ENIAC) Stw/Wikimedia Commons; p. 19 (main) ArnoldReinhold/Wikimedia Commons; p. 19 (inset) Rama/Wikimedia Commons; p. 21 Neirfy/Shutterstock.com.

All rights reserved. No part of this book may be reproduced in any form without permission in writing from the publisher, except by a reviewer.

Printed in the United States of America

CPSIA compliance information: Batch #CS15GS: For further information contact Gareth Stevens, New York, New York at 1-800-542-2595.

CONTENTS

Words in the glossary appear in **bold** type the first time they are used in the text.

DOES IT COMPUTE?

A computer is anything that counts, but **electronic** computers are what most people think of when you say "computer" today. They're in our homes, our cars, and even our pockets! The first true computers, however, could fill an entire room! Before that, computers could only do simple addition and subtraction.

Did you know the personal computer that's likely in your home is only a few decades old? Computers were built to count numbers more **accurately**, but there have been plenty of improvements made along the way.

OOPS!

As long as it can count, a "computer" can be made out of anything. In 1982, two scientists said they could make a computer out of billiard—or pool—balls!

COMPUTERS HAVE GOTTEN MUCH SMALLER AND MORE POWERFUL OVER THE LAST FEW DECADES.

5

COUNTING BOARDS AND THE ABACUS

Mathematics, or the science of numbers and how they relate, has changed and grown over thousands of years. One of the first tools used for math was called a counting board. It was a piece of wood, stone, or metal with places marked where pebbles went for counting.

The first abacus was made in China around 500 BC and used beads that were moved back and forth on a frame to count off numbers. This helped people count without using written **symbols** for each number.

OOPS!

Without tools like the abacus, people had to use their fingers and toes to count. They also used twigs and leaves to count higher numbers.

quipu, a system of knotted strings used by the Inca for computing

Chinese abacus

PASCAL'S CALCULATOR

Blaise Pascal was a French mathematician and scientist who made a calculator, or counting machine, used to work out math problems. In 1642, when Pascal was 18, he made the calculator to help his father calculate taxes.

His calculator used spoked wheels with numbers around each wheel to add numbers together. It could also be used for subtraction with a little bit of extra work. About 50 of these calculators were made. Pascal's first **design** had five wheels, but later designs had six and eight wheels.

OOPS!

Pascal made about 50 early designs of his calculator before settling on the spoked-wheel design he made famous.

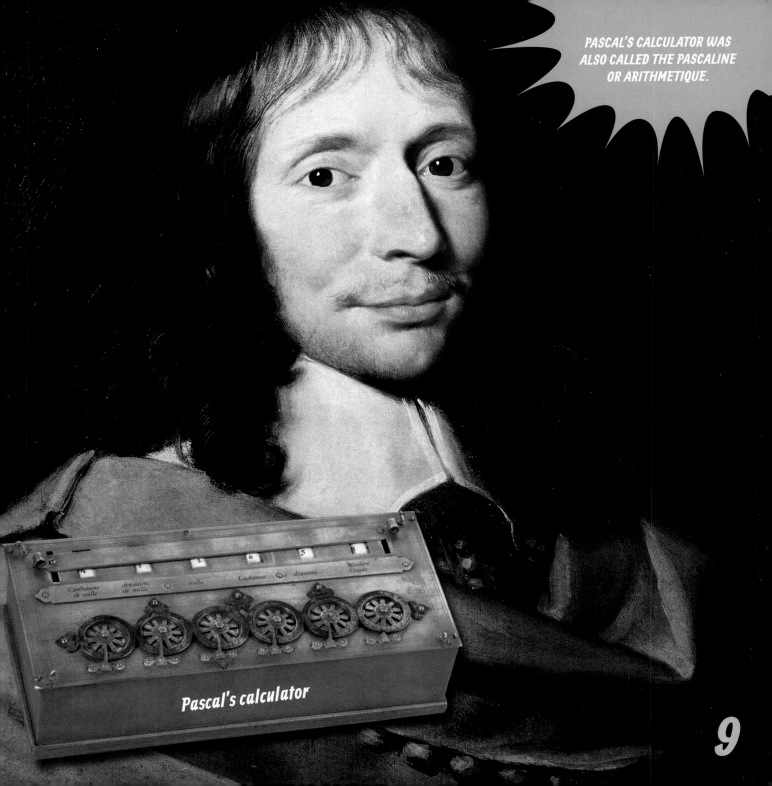

PASCAL'S CALCULATOR WAS ALSO CALLED THE PASCALINE OR ARITHMETIQUE.

Pascal's calculator

9

THE DIFFERENCE ENGINE

English mathematician and inventor Charles Babbage is often called the "father of computing." In 1821, Babbage invented a machine he called the Difference Engine No. 1. It was a calculator that used addition to complete math tables, but it was never finished.

He later wanted to make a machine that could do any kind of mathematical task. He designed this machine, called the **Analytical** Engine, in 1834. Babbage never built the Analytical Engine or his Difference Engine No. 2, which he also designed before his death in 1871.

OoPs!

Scientists in Britain finally completed the Difference Engine No. 2 in 1991, 120 years after Babbage's death.

Difference Engine No. 1

11

THE Z1

Many inventors tinkered with machines to carry out math problems throughout the 20th century. It wasn't until the 1930s that a machine was **programmable**. The Z1 was built in 1938 by German inventor Konrad Zuse.

The machine was given tasks through a punch tape reader. Punched tape is a strip of paper with holes in it that gives a computer **data**. Different punched tape would make the Z1 calculate different things, but it had no way of storing any data.

OOPS!
The Z1 was destroyed in the December 1943 bombing of Berlin during World War II (1939–1945).

ZUSE UPDATED THE DESIGNS FOR HIS COMPUTERS IN THE Z2 AND Z3, WHICH WERE SIMILAR TO HIS ORIGINAL DESIGN.

replica of Z3

replica of Zuse's Z1

13

CODEBREAKERS

During wartime, computers were used to make—and break—secret codes. To prevent enemies reading the messages they sent back and forth, armies used a **cipher** to hide their meaning. The German military used a machine called the Enigma machine, which could change ciphers each day with different coding wheels.

Britain built a machine called the Colossus to break German ciphers. Colossus could read 5,000 characters a second and helped Britain quickly crack German codes.

OOPS!

The **Allies** built 10 working Colossi, but they were destroyed and their designs were burned after World War II ended.

14

COMPARED TO MODERN
COMPUTERS, COLOSSUS WAS HUGE!
THE MACHINE WAS 7 FEET (2.1 M)
TALL, 17 FEET (5.2 M) WIDE, AND
11 FEET (3.4 M) DEEP.

ENIAC AND UNIVAC

The first general purpose computer, the Electronic Numerical Integrator and Computer, or ENIAC, was built in 1946. The ENIAC took up 18,000 square feet (1,672 sq m). It used nearly 18,000 vacuum tubes to compute numbers and perform other tasks.

The makers of the ENIAC later made the UNIVAC, the Universal Automatic Computer, in 1951. They started a business and sold 46 UNIVACs to different organizations, including the US government. It was 25 feet by 50 feet (7.6 m by 15.2 m) and used 5,600 vacuum tubes.

OoPs!

At least one vacuum tube, which turned on and off to complete electrical circuits, needed to be replaced every few days in the ENIAC. The people working on the machine had to change burned tubes quickly to keep the machine working.

ENIAC

IN 1952, A UNIVAC **PREDICTED** DWIGHT EISENHOWER'S SURPRISE BIG WIN IN THE PRESIDENTIAL ELECTION WITH ONLY A SMALL NUMBER OF VOTES OFFICIALLY COUNTED.

UNIVAC

central computer

UNISERVOs

supervisory control

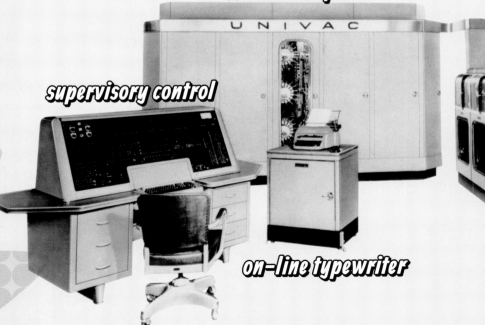

on-line typewriter

17

IBM SYSTEM/360

IBM made its own computer to compete with the UNIVAC in 1964. The IBM System/360 was called a mainframe, which is a large computer connected to other computers. Smaller computers, called workstations, could get the data held by mainframe computers and use it to perform other tasks.

The IBM System/360 was the first computer that could be upgraded, or made batter. Parts of the system could be changed out to make it faster without needing to buy a new computer.

oOPs!

IBM spent more than $5 billion making the IBM S/360. Buying a new S/360 cost about $2 million, so many companies could only rent them!

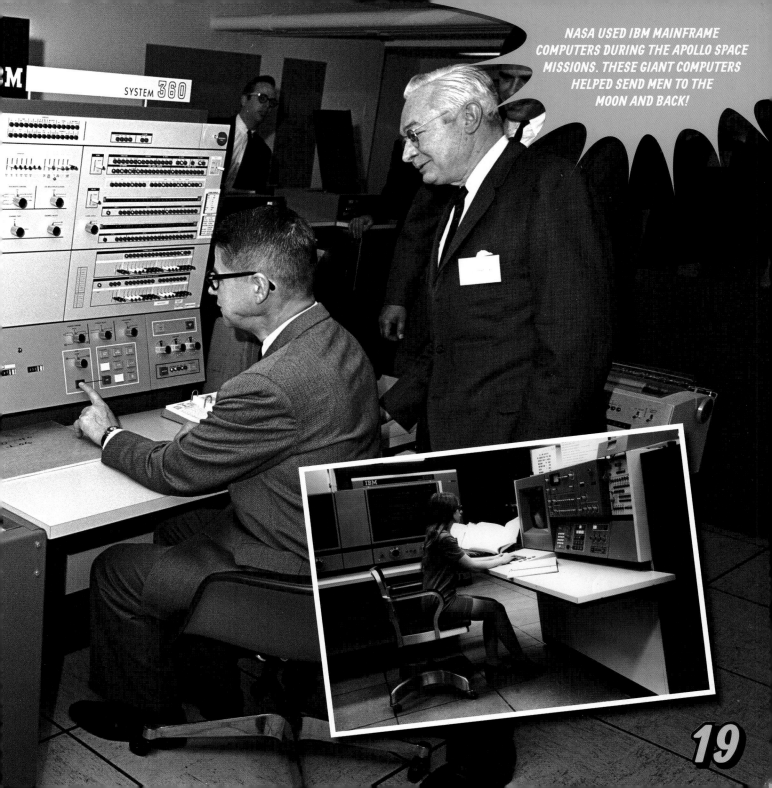

NASA USED IBM MAINFRAME COMPUTERS DURING THE APOLLO SPACE MISSIONS. THESE GIANT COMPUTERS HELPED SEND MEN TO THE MOON AND BACK!

19

PERSONAL COMPUTERS AND BEYOND

We've come a long way from massive machines built just to do math problems. IBM made the first personal computer, the Model 5150, in 1981. It didn't even have a mouse, which was made popular by Apple's Lisa 2 years later.

Computers quickly moved from science labs to homes around the world. Many now have touch screens and are small enough to sit on your lap. Even our cell phones are tiny computers much more powerful than the huge machines they grew out of.

OOPS!

One of the biggest problems with modern computers is that new technology moves too fast! Newer, smaller computers are always being made that make older machines **obsolete**.

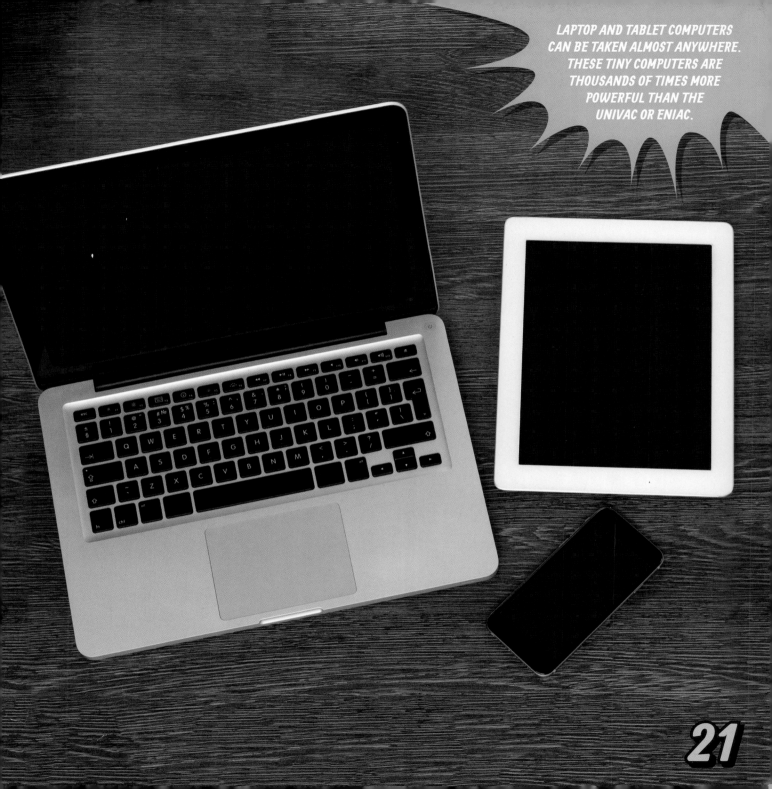

GLOSSARY

accurately: in such a way as to be free from mistakes

Allies: a group of countries that fought together in World War II including the United States, Soviet Union, and United Kingdom

analytical: having to do with separating something into its parts

cipher: a way of changing a message to hide its meaning

data: facts or numbers collected for further use

design: the pattern or shape of something. Also, to create the pattern or shape of something

electronic: powered by electricity

obsolete: no longer in style or use

predict: to guess what will happen in the future based on facts or knowledge

programmable: able to be made to do a specific task

symbol: a picture or shape that stands for something else

FOR MORE INFORMATION

BOOKS

Peterson, Megan Cooley. *The First Computers*. North Mankato, MN: Capstone Press, 2015.

Somervill, Barbara A. *The History of the Computer*. Chanhassen, MN: Child's World, 2006.

Weber, Rebecca. *Computers Then and Now*. Minneapolis, MN: Compass Point Books, 2005.

WEBSITES

Abacus and Its History
ucmas.ca/our-programs/how-does-it-work/abacus-and-its-history/
Find out more about the abacus, and see how it worked on this site.

Computers: History, Components and Future
easyscienceforkids.com/all-about-computers/
Learn more about the history of computers here.

Publisher's note to educators and parents: Our editors have carefully reviewed these websites to ensure that they are suitable for students. Many websites change frequently, however, and we cannot guarantee that a site's future contents will continue to meet our high standards of quality and educational value. Be advised that students should be closely supervised whenever they access the Internet.

INDEX